My Lost PAGES

SNEHA SABU

My Lost Pages
Sneha Sabu

Published by White Falcon Publishing
Chandigarh, India

All rights reserved
First Edition, 2024
© Sneha Sabu, 2024
Cover design concept by Sneha Sabu
Cover design by White Falcon Publishing, 2024
Cover image source freepik.com

The contents of this book have been certified and timestamped on
the POA Network blockchain as a permanent proof of existence.
Scan the QR code or visit the URL given on the back cover to
verify the blockchain certification for this book.

Contact the author at:
www.snehasabu.com

ISBN - 979-8-89222-169-6

About the Author

Sneha Sabu is an international strategist, development thinker, motivational speaker and author. Born and brought up in Kerala, the southern state of India known as 'God's Own Country,' Sneha has worked to improve the life of communities in 18 countries across the Asia Pacific region. In 2021, Sneha Sabu received the 'International Achievers' Award', 'Bharath Gaurav Puraskar' and 'The Real Superwoman Award'. In 2020, her biography was included In Marquis Who's Who in America. In 2019-20, she was listed in Marquis Who's Who in the World, inclusion in which is limited to individuals who possess professional integrity, demonstrate outstanding achievement in their respective fields and make exceptional contributions to society.

Sneha has written more than 25 short stories for children, 45 poems, and articles on social issues. Sneha is a writer of freestyle poetry and is passionate about contemporary and abstract concepts, emotional and humane elements, social and environmental issues. Sneha's notable work Stay Safe with Ruby and Rueben is an earnest effort to create awareness among children on child safety and how to protect children from child sexual abuse. Stay Safe with Ruby and Reuben won multiple international awards and recognitions including the BREW Reader's Choice of the Year 2023, the BREW Book Excellence Award 2023 Winner in Children's Activity Book category, the 2023 Independent Publisher Book Awards Bronze Winner in Children's Interactive, the 2023 Purple Dragonfly Book Award Honorable Mention in Global and Social Issues category, the May 2022 International Impact Award, and the Story Monsters Book Award Winner in 2022 Education/Reference Category.

Sneha invites you to visit her at www.snehasabu.com.

This book is dedicated to

GOD, my father, without whom
I will not be what I am today,
my mother Sudha, who encouraged me all my life,

AND

hubby Vinu and brother Cyriack – the people
who will kill me if they are not acknowledged.

Disclaimer

This book is a collection of poems of different styles. The author recognises and respects the traditional owners and custodians of all lands mentioned in these poems. The author believes in the equal, fair and just treatment of humankind, regardless of background, gender, cultural and socio-economic orientation.

This book contains information that may be considered sensitive and offensive for some readers. The language of the poems reflects artistic expression and is not, by any means, intended to offend anyone; reader discretion is advised.

Table of Contents

1. Carbon

My granny made halwas
In brass woks over fire lit with coal.
In hues of green, orange and black,
The aroma filled the room.
The coal added to the unique flavour
Of halwas we ate day and night.
My cousins and I rushed
To taste the halwas before they cooled.
With time, she switched to electricity
When power failed,
We were back to coal.
Barbeque did she tapiocas in coal,
Gather did we
For a char-grilled feast.
The dark coal
Sat on an outdoor veranda
With no one paying heed
Unless it rained.
We threw cold coal into the earthen pots
Where nested my mother's plants –
Anthuriums and orchids.
As they grew and flourished,
We credited the coal.
That eve the electricity man came home,
I learned a new lesson.

The first steam engine,
Electricity, were all gifts of coal.
Then came the grandeur,
Coal's cousin, the diamond.
The most expensive gift
I ever received.
From that day
I looked at coal,
With more awe and love.
As spring bloomed,
Flowers blossomed,
My canvas stretched.
I made the finest masterpiece
With a piece of charcoal;
For in coal, charcoal and diamond
And in humans and my masterpiece
Is carbon in all its forms.

Inspiration or thought: Carbon

Carbon exists in different forms and shapes. They are like humans; the more pressure the carbon withstands, the more it evolves and transforms into something beautiful. Our life experiences and responses to these situations mould us into the different forms of carbon we are. Carbon exists in coal, charcoal, diamonds and humans in varying porcontages. Under varied environmental conditions, they evolve into what they are meant to be.

2. Dew Drops

The visitors landed at night
Ready to slide down the velvety leaves.
Some caught in the blossomed autumn petals,
Some stood by the lake, ready for a fall.

At the break of dawn,
The water pearls rolled down
Like two dancers swirling their skirts
As they kissed the lake.

Short-lived, the pearls' gentle touch
Made the berry bloom;
Waiting for the sunlight
To sparkle like a diamond.

White dahlia stood like a grand sculpture
Straining for a glimpse in those curvy faces.
The group swayed in the wind
As they mirrored on a row of pearls.

As the ray of first sunshine
Broke the dawn
The pearl drops scattered colours of rainbow
Like a precious diamond that caught interest.

Inspiration or thought:
Dew Drops

Dew drops are tiny droplets of water that play a crucial role in sustaining our ecosystem. Some plants can survive in drought-like conditions only because dew drops give them life. It is incredible how nature works to sustain Earth's flora and fauna!

3. Down Memory Lane

In the quirky corridor, I stand,
Gazing at the frames
That hold my story;
Of travel, love and romance,
Of adventure, fun and frolic.
Photos of tales and experiences,
Some spoken, some silent,
Held close to my heart.
In the corridor of my daily walk
I leave them hanging
To submerge me in nostalgia
Of memories far and near.
Every guest did gaze for a second or two
As I straightened up in pride,
Narrating the tales behind them.
Travelled did I far and wide
Hopping from
One country to another.
My hair found a new friend –
A friend called grey,
The grey of wisdom.
Time dulled my memory,
The resilience and energy
Is far off the bay.

These photos tell tales:
The Hawaiian sun
With a flower on my head;
The Vegas dreams of youth,
Paragliding thrills in New Zealand,
Where the mesmerising beauty of nature
Bunched my cheeks;
The moment well-captured.
Relive did they
Through the photos
Hung in my quirky corridor.

Inspiration or thought:
Down Memory Lane

"Down Memory Lane" is a journey through one's memories. In our busy day-to-day lives, we often forget to stop and cherish the beautiful moments. Yet, when we take a moment to stop and look at the photographs hung in our corridors, they take us to a joyful and distinct world of memories. These memories become sweeter in times they seem too distant to be revisited.

4. From the Ashes I Rise

By the beach I stand
With the rushing waves of reminders
Of being born brown
In a discriminatory world.

I have layers of melanin,
More than shades of
White, pink and green,
Enough to shade my eyes and skin brown.

Like a gatherer
Did I wander in search of food and shelter,
For the colour of my skin
Fetched me no job nor food.

I stand in line,
Am asked to wait and wait;
Not offered a seat to sit,
Not allowed to eat from the same plate
Or be together with the rest of the group.

I am not alone
In this colour of race;
The struggles are dying
For the collective voice is growing.

The voice of rebellion is soaring:
A voice of equality, fairness
And just treatment of the human race.

Cultures penetrated;
So did neo-colonialism.
The ape is evolving
To be *Homo sapiens* of equality.

Inspiration or thought: From the Ashes I Rise

We enter into the world nude and leave the world nude. We have all evolved from the apes. We are a part of a species called *Homo sapiens*. However, people are discriminated against in different forms across the world. The fight for equality is an ongoing struggle that has led to rebellions and movements. A world of equality is still distant, and it is a goal that demands urgent action.

5. Have Some Mercy on Me

My head feels light
Tummy loose
My stool green
The takeaway took a toll.
My home nurse
Cleaned my poop
Her rough hands moved me to the side
Her eyes gave me a look of empathy.
I smiled within!
How would she even know what this means?
To lie paralysed on my death bed!
They think my end is near
My body cannot move
It is frozen
They follow no diet
For when a man leaves the earth
He gets to eat what he wants.
In the days of my youth
The fitness mania got into me
I ate nothing but greens and organic food
As age-sprouted diabetes set in
The diet worsened so I could stay fitter.
Not a flab or pot belly did I see
I saw my family feast day and night
While I sat in the corner with a bowl of veggies.

One day of carelessness on the road
Cost me my life.
Today I lie paralysed!
It has not been a day or two
It's been a decade
Bed sores are bursting;
At times they bleed.
My family feeds me everything
Hoping when the end is near
I may die in luxury.
In hope of an easy death
I lie months and years
Years keep passing,
But in no hope I lie.
With no sign of recovery,
My mind is alert,
Body dead.
My tongue is numb
I hope for some mercy every day
A mercy to take my life.
Humanity does not let the family kill
Ethical codes stop the doctor
Termites are eating the wood in my house
No one cares
For they are all here for the day of my funeral.
This time around, the hope is sky high.
Nor will they grant me a merciful death
Nor will they let me lie in peace
I am cleaned and wiped
To look beautiful for the funeral service.

The monthly ordeal of hope continued
And continued.
I still lie in hope
Of a doctor or family mercy killing me
For all our sakes!

Inspiration or thought:
Have Some Mercy on Me

Even if we lead the healthiest life, it takes only a split second to turn our lives upside down. Even in the most adverse situations, mercy killing is not accepted in most countries. When one is alive but cannot move an inch, one is in constant search of mercy. Some would have a tiny little hope that they may recover. Others may be ready to leave. Living life to the fullest is vital so that we have good memories to cherish when circumstances change.

6. Hey Fish!

Hey Fish!
Don't you be afraid
The boat is nearing the shore
You are the best catch of the day.

Hey Fish!
Don't you be afraid
Men and women are eyeing you
You are the star of the morning sale.

Hey Fish!
Don't you be afraid
The seafood store paid a fortune
You are their favourite pick of the day.

Hey Fish!
Don't you be afraid
The sharpest knife will make your cutlets
You will die a death of dignity today.

Hey Fish!
Don't you be afraid
Your cutlets are priced high
You sit at the front of the display like a piece of gold.

Hey Fish!
Don't you be afraid
Here comes the Thai lady
You will make fish larb with lemon and herbs tonight!

Hey Fish!
Don't you be afraid
Here comes the Aussie bloke
You are going to be sizzling on his grill tonight!

Hey Fish!
Don't you be afraid
Your last cutlet is going to an Indian home
You will swim in masala to make the best fish fry of the day!

Inspiration or thought:
Hey Fish!

Fish forms an integral part of most cuisines. When a fish is caught in a net for the first time, it would undoubtedly be stressed. Like any other animal, the fish deserves to be killed humanely, in a stress-free manner, for consumption. Until the fish is stunned, it deserves to be in the water. The author gives fish a death of dignity by letting the best stunners stun the fish. The fish is treated with respect and admiration for what it offers.

7. Lake Tekapo

The starlit sky
Kissed the snowy mountains
The glacier lake of South
Mirrored the sky
The snowy sheet of the mountain ranges
Mirrored in its still water.
Mount Cook smiled
As he saw the stars
At his foothills.
The fine snow blankets
Slid down the ranges
To fill the aquamarine lake.
The hue stilled the breath
Of every onlooker
The sky was cloudless
The wild flowering lupins
Laid a bed for the tourists.
Pink and purple flowers swayed with the wind
In the dark night.
The rustic Good Shepherd Church
Stood on its tiny stone structure
By the shore of the lake.

The night is calm and still
The Tekapo springs silent
I could hear no steps
The scent of blooming flowers
Filled the air.
An artist's stroke
Perfect in all seasons
Lake Tekapo is a marvel
Of the South Island.

Inspiration or thought: Lake Tekapo

Situated in the South Island, New Zealand, Lake Tekapo is a visual treat. What makes Lake Tekapo unique is the colour of its water and its picturesque beauty. It is close to the Southern Alps, a favourite holiday spot, and it stands to mesmerise in all seasons. In November and December, lupins grow around the lake. In winter, tho snow sheets slide down to add to the colour of the water.

8. My Big Fat Bum

I climbed the weighing scale,
The scale did not break
To my surprise!
There were bigger scales
That could hold weight beyond mine.
Morbidly Obese!
The doctor claimed.
My wide smile dimmed
I know I am obese
But morbid is melancholic.
My bum is big and round
It added to most of my weight.
My mom and dad have big bums
So do my aunts.
But mine is the biggest of the lot.

I got on the plane back home.
A wedding awaited
The cheap plane ticket came with a price
I knew not!
The seat of aluminium
Looked nice and attractive
But the armrest framed the seat
Leaving me hardly any room
To fit my bum in!

With no choice
I pushed my bum in
To fit into the tiny little space.

My bum suffocated
It pleaded for some circulation.
My bum was numb.
The pressure built in
No air to breathe
The numbness painful
The eight-hour long flight
Turned into joyless agony.
I tucked my bum in and out
To release some pressure
Eight hours was too long
To keep this pressure game going.

The wedding bells rang
I dressed up, danced and partied
As I reached the groom's house,
Nature called
I ran to the restroom.
As I sat
The toilet shook
I heard a creaky noise
Bang! The water closet fell apart
I was on the floor
With part of my bum
Stuck between the broken pieces
The first night was at the hospital
With my bum sore with stitches.

I still love my bum
The doctor, the closet, the plane
Nothing changed my love.
As years passed,
I lived in a rented house
On the first floor.
My maid came to clean my balcony;
With soap and water, she soaked the place
My veggie vendor called from down the stairs
I ran out to take the stairs
The soap and water slid me down
My back hit every step
For the slippery floor
Gave me a ride.
My bum cushioned my spine
From a crack and a spine injury.

Inspiration or thought: My Big Fat Bum

We all come in different shapes and sizes. Quite often, obese people are body-shamed in several societies. Despite the challenges, everyone's body is unique and different. Embracing ourselves for what we are is most important to be happy. Some people may work out for several hours to remain in shape, but they may miss out on some goodies that others enjoy. People with bigger bodies may have their own challenges as well. The most important factor, whatever be your body type, is to love yourself.

9. My Mirror Reflection

At dusk and dawn
In the dim moonlight
In the misty mornings
Not a day nor night passed
Without a glance at my mirror.
As I grew older,
The gazing grew too.
I felt beautiful,
The more I gazed.
As years passed,
A strand of grey shocked me.
If not for the mirror
I could not have realised
How obese I had become.
Every diet day
I gazed and gazed
At every flab and love handle
In hope of losing them.
Some days
The gaze made me happy,
Other days sad.
My mirror taught and trained me,
To smile when I am sad.
My brain played tricks on me
The more I gazed
Creepier and weirder I seemed.

I gazed to see
How far my tears ran down my cheeks
But the more I gazed
A smile sprouted on my face.
I knew what I was
For my mirror reflected
The true me.

Inspiration or thought: The Mirror Reflection

A mirror reflects any object in front of it in the most identical manner. However, it offers a reversed image. Despite these slight differences, our facial expressions and emotions are reflected on its surface in the best possible manner. A mirror reflects our true identity, which is often masked in an open environment.

10. Paranormal

A horror movie kept our droopy eyes still.
With one eye open
I saw the bloodshed
We shook on the couch.
The street is empty
There are no cars
The air whistled around,
The cricket chirped.
Cold and numb we became
The cold air of fear ran down our spines.
In fear, the washroom visit skipped,
We ran together into the bedroom
Switching off the lights on the way.
The bedroom blinds left wide open
The lights from the building opposite
Lit the night.
As lights went off
Insomnia set in.
The killer haunted us
Through the night.
Our clock kept ticking
The second's needle
Moved like an albatross round our neck.
The clock struck eleven
An hour to midnight!

Our phones lay charging
Next to the television in the living room
As time passed, a tiny nap kissed us
At 11.59 pm, we woke up in fear
A melancholy did we hear –
A song of the past.
Louder and louder, it played
The television was off
The phone far away
What is that?
We jumped off our bed
We looked at each other.
A song we played several months back
But, nothing was left on.
Half asleep, did I have more courage
Walked I did into the living room
To see my hubby's phone
Playing music on its own.
The clock struck 12.00 as the music played!

Inspiration or thought:
Paranormal

This poem is based on a real-life incident, as experienced by the author. When one goes to sleep after watching a horror movie, an unsaid fear remains with some people. At times, it prompts one to construe a natural event as paranormal.

11. Shakespeare's Knight

The moon smiled at the water beneath the bridge
The knight came riding on his horse
The city was asleep
The princess could not sleep.
She heard the knight on the horse
Clip-clop!! The horse galloped
To her castle.
She waited day and night
For her knight.
Shakespearean aura filled her reading
Valliant and chivalrous
A title of honour and pride
In service of the crown
For her knight.
The modern princess read to her fallacy,
For a knight she wanted to marry
To honour the knights of Shakespeare.
The glorious title did wane
The knight had no horse left
The knight lives in books
Far from the days
Of Shakespeare.
The princess lived in her fantasy
Waiting for her knight
She waited by the window side
For the knight to come galloping on his horse.

As the city slept
For the busy day that followed
The knight came on his horse
To take the princess away.
Wait did she
Live did she
Through the life of her Shakespearean knight.
The wait fulfilled
When the knight on his horse
Climbed the ladder placed against her castle
And took her away.

Inspiration or thought: Shakespeare's Knight

Traditionally, knights held a noble rank. They were trained to fight chivalrously and bravely to protect the crown. The knights in literature were always a fantasy for women. The knights demonstrated strong virtues of kindness, mercy, courage, sacrifice and honour.

12. *Surviving the Pandemic*

Prison did fascinate me
For I knew not what it entailed;
The four walls of the cellar
Suffocated me from a distance.
Read did I with fascination
About the pandemic of 1869,
Of what life could have been.
152 years did we wait
To revisit the yesteryears
Of souls that survived the pandemic.
Stuck on an island
Surrounded by water
We dwelt in a beautiful land
We called paradise on earth.
The virus broke the walls we mended
And disparities we set;
It travelled far and near
To every house known
And every country known.
We stayed at home
Binge watching and ordering food for delivery
The social bee in me
Felt lonely and lost.
We masked our faces
Leaving just our eyes to see the world.

Virtual reallly set in
With no one to join in a meal
Or have a drink with.
With gyms and pools locked up
In pyjamas we stayed day and night.
Splashed did I some make up on my face;
With a decent-looking top
And shabby trousers,
For what the camera picked up
Was my face and my shoulders.
We prayed for healing
Appreciated the lorikeet and magpie that passed
We draped the balcony with patches of green
My friends read and read
I wrote and wrote
For we wanted to occupy our minds
In a frozen world.
Some did die
Other did heal
The vaccines did come
With side effects for some.
Friends and families were aloof
For all we spoke was of what we could not do.
Weddings were on hold
Economy on a stand still
Healing is slow
We geared up for a new world;
A world of social distancing and restrictions
A world of the vaccinated and the unvaccinated
A world of new order.

We are ready with a new ray of hope
Where freedom has a new meaning
And relationships new boundaries
The pandemic did teach us a lot.
That life can go on
With rules, boundaries and things we can't forego.
For a world of new truths, realities and visions
We are ready
For being human has a new meaning.

We are ready with a new ray of hope
Where freedom has a new meaning
And relationships new boundaries
The pandemic did teach us a lot.
That life can go on
With rules, boundaries and things we can't forego.
For a world of new truths, realities and visions
We are ready
For being human has a new meaning.

Inspiration or thought: Surviving the Pandemic

The COVID-19 pandemic transformed the world in different ways. We realised that we can, indeed, survive without several things we had earlier considered indispensable. Despite the challenges it brought in, it made people more creative. When we were all stuck at home, we had time to spend with family - either to make up for lost time or to finish the pending quarrels. We saw the best and the worst of the world, which transformed our perspectives. Personally, I appreciate every small living thing I saw during the lockdown, including the spider that encroached into my balcony patch.

13. *The Bee and the Fly*

In hues of gold and onyx
I flew from one flower to another
From wild purple poppies to red roses
Did I gather honey for our comb.

I laboured day and night
For my wax
Made a beautiful cell
For the Queen of my life.

I sat in Uncle Blake's garden,
The mango tree by the aloe
Is my new home.
I, the bee, buzzed and there came my friends.

The pleasure to gather honey was mine
The generosity of the poppies and the roses noteworthy,
For the affair was two-sided
I carried their pollen from one to another.

In gratitude did they sway
And so did I buzz in gratitude

My friend the little fly
Waited till summer
To dance and sing around
Until Uncle Blake brushed him off.

The little fly bumped on the floor and woke up
It flew in giddy circles
It crossed the garden,
The poppies and the roses.

The little fly would never stop by
For the floral scents won't attract him
It flew around
In search of dirt and filth.

Inspiration or thought: The Bee and the Fly

The bee and the fly fall into the insect category. What makes the bee interesting is its ability to gather honey from flowers without distorting it. It plays a role in pollination as well. However, unlike the bee, no matter how beautiful the world is, the fly is always searching for filth and dirt. As humans, we have a choice – to coexist like the bee or to be filled with filth like the fly.

14. The Blue Woman

It is a baby girl!
Let us get her pink dress,
Dolls and Barbies
For she is a beauty!
I am born a human,
Not pink or blue.
You tagged me pink,
And tried moulding me to be as pink as you wanted.
My brains are like a man
My physique like a woman.
I fought my battles to study,
And to be the woman I am.
The streets of my life are dark,
Women can't walk at night
They are raped, abused and molested.
We speak of independence, rights and equality.
What is freedom if a woman cannot dream?
Is stuck as her man's maid,
And is a victim of violence and abuse?
Where are her rights if she does not have a voice?
To speak and be the person she wants to be?
If she speaks, she is an activist or a feminist
If she wears clothes off the norm,
She is cultureless and uncivilised.
If she is obese, she can't find a man;
She is asked to lose weight to be in a relationship.

If she is barren, she is ill-treated all her life
If she bore a girl, she is questioned.
A man holds the gender in his chromosome
A woman bears the pain and delivers.

I am a woman
And am proud to be one
I like blue, and that is my colour.
I hate pink, and that is my choice.
I may have a peg, wear shorts and a bikini,
And that is my choice.
I may walk the dark streets at night
But that does not give a man the freedom
To touch me without my consent,
To abuse or molest me.
Here I am, a blue woman.
Who thinks like a man,
Wears the clothes of her choice,
Fights for her voice, independence and rights.
And this fight is not a solo fight,
It is a battle for every woman
Who deserves to be the person
She wants to be.

Inspiration or thought:
The Blue Woman

"The Blue Woman" is the voice of the suppressed, abused and stereotyped women from the communities where gender equality and treatment of women with dignity and respect is still a work in progress. The voice raises the need for acceptance and equality and the need to break norms to make the world a better and safer place for women – a place where they can be what they want to be.

15. The Change Warrior

White clouds filled the clear sky
The brown- and white-headed eagle circled
Round and round.
A prey laid ready for its talons
Beneath the mangrove.
From my balcony did I watch
The eagle perching
Several feet above.
I thought I lived high enough,
The eagle flew higher.
The eagle waited and waited
Calm and patient
To snatch the baby rabbit.
Like a swift she flew closer and closer
To the baby rabbit.
Alas! She snatched the baby rabbit
And flew far away.
With mighty claws and beak
She came on and off
To snatch a prey or two.
Years passed,
My hair grew grey
The eagle grew grey with me.
I felt I had company
For the eagle could snatch no more.

I waited for It to perch;
She stopped coming.
Far away, on the mountain
By a rock she stayed.
She pecked and pecked her beak
Against the strong rock
Until the beak broke.
The eagle stood up beakless
In patience did it wait,
For the new beak did grow
Day by day.
I showed off my new hair colour
A cover for my age.
The eagle plucked off its feathers and talons
And showed off no beak to the world.
The talons grew stronger
So did the new feathers and beak.
The eagle was young again
Strong and mighty like a young warrior
Ready for war.
I sat amazed
As the eagle came back
Age never stood in its way
For it was young again
To snatch its prey
A lesson I did learn
From the eagle mighty and young
A lesson of change and adaptation
To be what you need to be
For survival comes with the price of change
In a changing world.

Inspiration or thought:
The Change Warrior

The eagle is a very motivational bird. It lives for up to 80 years. As it reaches 40, its beak, talons and feathers grow old. Age makes it hard for the eagle to hunt down its prey. It would fly to a quiet spot and break its beak. As the new beak grows, it plucks off its feathers and talons. The new beak, talons and feathers make the eagle mighty and strong. The eagle exhibits an example of adaptation to change.

16. The File in the Bin

In your recycle bin I lie
Like any other file
Ignored with other junk.
I travelled from one inbox to another
Was loved and cared for
When I was new.
New concepts and versions
Have come in;
Now I am outdated.
Like the clutter in a garbage bin
I lie in your recycle bin
All it takes is a click
I keep pondering: Why is it taking so long?
For a click on the restore button
Can change my life,
Bring back my old name and fame.
What if you are dated?
Will your family bin you?
What if your new car gives you trouble?
Won't you repair and revive?
Ready to transform and change, I lie
To be a new edition or a version of your choice

For life in the recycle bin on your screen
Is dull and boring;
For I deserve to live a good life,
If not in your desktop glory
A life in archive glory!

Inspiration or thought:
The File in the Bin

We live in a fast-paced world where we are constantly upgrading our products. New versions are replacing old versions. There was a time when we used to repair and reuse products, thus increasing their overall life span. Consumerism is a tenet of the modern world. However, this lifestyle is also translated into the way we treat people. As people age, they are ignored within the households, and some are sent to old age homes or retirement villages.

17. The Loan Shark

For want of a house
I met the bank manager.
For want of a better space
I got my grandpa's and mom's will.
I asked for an amount
They said they needed to check
They visited and visited
And asked for documents and documents.
I produced one after the other
But that was not it!
The officer needed a tip;
A bit more than a restaurant tip,
But he did not want to call it a bribe.
The paperwork was done
The loan was ready for approval
Then came the 'Man of the Match' –
The Regional Manager!
The paper game recommenced
For want of a home
I got them all again.
For want of a better space
I produced one after the other.
But that was not it!
He asked for more and more.

The ordeal took days and months
Emotional and shattered was I
For I saw no light.
I was on the verge –
The verge of giving up.
The end of year targets neared
The manager was under pressure
So was the Regional Manager!
A call came two days before the year end:
'Your loan is approved!'
I had pending papers to submit
And now that was not required!
When I thought the ordeal was over
There came a catch.
'You need to pay us extra
For releasing the amount before year end.'
I was happy to wait for two days,
For the year end was but two days away.
The man pushed and pushed
Called and called
Emailed and emailed
I stood firm with a 'No!'
He waived the fee
To meet his target
And let me off the hook –
With a huge monthly EMI on my shoulders!

Inspiration or thought:
The Loan Shark

We are living in an era where mortgages or loans are part of everyone's lives. In some societies, the common person is forced to struggle through long-winded processes to get a loan approved, even when they have all the required documents intact. People often opt for loans to ease the burden of a financial predicament. People are already under stress when they apply for a loan. The poem is based on a real-life situation faced by an individual when she applied for a loan. The poem is intended to depict the struggles faced at a particular instance and is not to be misunderstood as a societal or collective stereotype.

18. The Nourishing Hump

Like a camel, I too carry a hump –
The baggage of finding the meaning of human existence.
The load is heavy
Not with chores or labour
But with finding meaning and purpose.
The hump does nourish me
With tales of yore
When times are hard and heavily laden.
The brain and heart are in conflict
So are the voices of the soul.
'What am I here for?' the brain pondered.
'To help others,' the heart chuckled.
'If I am to help others, what are others for?'
My brain questioned and questioned
The left and right brain swayed in thought
The heart joined the discussion.
Why do I think?
Why can't I just do?
Why can't I think *and* do?
Boundaries did I maintain
To keep filthy mouths at bay
The pleasures of the world
Do I cherish.

My soul wants a meaningful life
My mind a happy life
The body a fun-filled life to enjoy this world
My spirit wants it all.
Life on earth is a gift
A gift that lasts a lifetime
Let your heart, brain and mind ponder.
In search of meaning my soul suffocates
I let the brain, heart and soul indulge
In the life I live; it is their right.
So is it my right to choose whom to listen to.
As years add to my life
So does the depth of my thought
The hump grows bigger and larger
As age sets in.
For all my thoughts,
I may not have answers.
As years pass, memory fades from the brain
The pleasure of the body dies
The heart finds no meaning
The voices of the soul may not have energy to fight.
In the blossoming youth
Let it all ponder and sway!
Let the rhythm of life
Play music over its course,
For the spirit needs it all
In all phases of its life!

Inspiration or thought: The Nourishing Hump

There will come a time in some of our lives when we question the reason for our existence. We tend to question everything around us to find the true meaning of existence. Our mind, body, heart, soul and spirit work in an integrated manner. But as we contemplate about existence and more profound meaning, the way we hear our inner voice changes. Navigating through this introspection is an enriching experience.

19. The Room that Saved!

The bumpy road shook my bladder
As the rickshaw drove us to the mall.
My window shopper cousin
Browsed and browsed through every shop.
She did not buy a thing
Nor did she let me buy a meal.

Hours passed.
My bladder is full
I was stuck with my cousin
In a store hidden in the mall corridor.
My eyes blurred,
For my bladder could not hold on.
I kept walking towards the exit;
She drew me back
To take a look at a new collection.

I need to pee!
Hold on. Let's go after this store.
I kept peeping through the glass panes
In the hope of finding the sign boards:
The blue and white neon-lit
Men and women in a box;
That was all that my eyes wanted to see.

Madam, can I show you our new collection?
Where is the loo?
You mean rest room?
Whatever you call it!
There is one just behind.
Where is it?
Guests are not allowed
Then why say there is one,
When I can't use this one!
The lady smiled.
There is one for the public down the escalator.

I ran to my cousin
I want to go now!
My voice tough,
She knew I meant business.
Can't you wait for some more time?
I can't wait a sec
Come with me now.

Oh! Is it that urgent?
You could have said.
Well, why wait for me
Just go help yourself!
You kept holding me back!
Oh, did I?
It's your bladder, you should have known better!
I am going now.

The room laughed as I dashed out
In the hope of finding the loo
I sprinted down the escalator
I felt snails were faster than these!
I ran and ran around the mall
Until I found the board
With the blue and white neon light –
With a man and woman framed within.

At last! I thought
I entered a narrow alley
From there to another
From there to another
From one lane to another
It took me seven minutes to reach the loo!
But when I reached,
A battalion was waiting in queue!

Ladies! I want to pee!
So do we!
It is urgent
It will drop down any second
Can I go next?
An old woman paved the way
I rushed to my favourite room of the day!
My blurry eyes cleared up
As I peed down the drain.

Inspiration or thought:
The Room that Saved!

Going to the restroom when you feel like it is an integral part of how the human body works. At times, to be polite and courteous, we hold in our basic needs. Going to the restroom is one such need. The discomfort caused by such an action is indescribable. If you feel it, you should do it! If you hold it in out of courtesy, you are disrupting your system, which could result in bladder disorders and other health issues.

20. The Shooting Star

Clothed in radiance
The night sky stood
Diamond-studded.
Light years away
Do they stand,
Filled with helium and hydrogen.
From nebulae do they come
And live billions of years.

Like a sister star
Does the rock shoot out
And fly down to the earth
From space.
Like Mockingjay
They burn alive
Before their souls
Touch the ground.

The layperson's wish star
Astronomers' meteor.
A sign of hope and positivity,
The Shooting Star
Heats up and glows.
Like a swift it flies
To torch the sky and the earth.

Inspiration or thought:
The Shooting Star

A starlit sky is a visual treat for the onlooker. A quick study into astronomy would reveal the science behind the existence of stars and associated phenomena. Their origin is complex and it narrates a tale of evolution. What makes the night beautiful is the very existence of these stars. The shooting star is different from the rest of the stars we see. In many cultures, they are seen as a positive sign. Though we see a swift-moving star like a blazing torch, the shooting 'star' is really a meteor that burns up when it enters the earth's atmosphere.

21. The Wild Fire

The earth cracked from the scotching heat
Kangaroos hopped from the bush and onto the roads
The forest lake dried up
The wild fire spread through the ranges and valleys.

The fire kept spreading and spreading
The possums, wombats and kangaroos ran and hopped;
But the fire was faster
It swept and engulfed them all.

The fire surrounded our house.
Every tree caught fire
The barks were charred black,
My dad's boat caught fire.

I hid in Nana's closet
I always hide when fear crawls in.
I am scared;
I don't want to die.

Dad and Mom is out of town
I am all alone with Nana.
People said wooden houses catch fire
Stephanie! Stephanie! We need to go!
The fire reached our kitchen.

We were ready to fly like a bird
The house was on fire
The woods were on fire
Our animals were on fire.
Nana and I got into the car;
We were safe.
We kept driving and driving –
The fire caught up.

We drove and drove,
The fire chased us.
We kept driving – proud – we beat the fire!
The fire subdued us from the front.
Our car was on fire
We were lit up by the fire.

Inspiration or thought:
The Wild Fire

The wild fire is an unplanned fire in the bushes that spreads at a breakneck pace. In summer, one should be very cautious about the fire. When emergency services issue an evacuation warning, it is our collective responsibility to respond and adhere to them. Ignoring the warnings and delayed evacuations have lost many lives to wild fires around the world.

22. *The Woodcutter's Son*

My dad was delighted at the news
My mom is three months pregnant!
My tiny body clung to my mother's womb
As my parents celebrated.

Dad wanted to make more money,
For money fetched a better life
For the little boy
In his wife's womb.

He left for our family house
In the forest;
He cut wood
And sold the logs.

The more money he earned,
The more trees he cleared.
The birds and animals
Lost their homes.

One day Mom joined Dad.
I was hurt to see
My village barren
My woodpecker, parakeet and lorikeets had lost their home.

My dad touched my mom's tummy –
I am doing this for him!
I want him to have a better morrow!
A better life than mine.
I kicked my dad's hand in anger
Look! He is moving.
He seems to be happy
My dad felt my leg.

My mom's heart burdened, so did mine.
We shifted to the village
Dad sold our land
To build a factory.

His eyes turned green with greed.
The factory was set;
It released toxins and chemicals
Into the air and the lake.

Day and night
My mother inhaled the poisonous air
Water from the lake did we drink
With all its chemicals.

My tiny body
Could not bear the toxins
I died in my mom's womb.
My dad's greed killed me, my trees and my birds!

Inspiration or thought:
The Woodcutter's Son

Our existence is a gift of nature. We are part of a broader ecosystem and food chain. The plants supply us oxygen and fresh air; the trees protect us from soil erosion. Nature plays a significant role in making our life better on Earth. In our greed, if we destroy the nature around us, we and the generations to come will bear the brunt.

23. *Things that Make me Laugh*

Stuffed with potatoes we made rotis
To give our guest a feast –
A feast filled with diary, gluten and carbs.
Overloaded on love,
Our tummies were full and bigger.

As we tucked in our blankets
After a 'Goodnight!' to our guests,
I heard a big long burp
From the guest room next doors.

The wind in the tummy and upper intestine
Was playing up and down,
For the guests had had
Heavy meals and aerated beverages
Topped with loads of ice.

Giggled did I with no empathy
For I was passing wind
From my bottom
That lasted few seconds like a drum roll.

After hours of sleeplessness
I ran to the corridor
To grab my gastro med.
As the capsule ran down my throat,
There came a hand asking for one.

The host-guest duo walked back to their rooms
With a sigh of relief
With the hope of catching a wink of sleep
Before the break of dawn.

As I latched my door,
A whistle did I hear.
I stopped to look through the windows
To find none.
In dismay did I look around
To find where the whistle came from.

My cousin did share my room that night.
As I walked to my bed
The whistle came closer and closer –
The sleeping cousin was snoring with a whistle.

A few minutes later I heard
A truck changing gears
My sharp ears pricked
To hear a gear-changing snore from the guest room.

Inspiration or thought:
Things that Make me Laugh

Passing wind and burping are two things that everyone does. It happens in the large intestine when food does not digest well in the small intestine. It comes out in the form of gas or a burp. On the other hand, snoring occurs when breathing is obstructed in sleep. While these are all natural phenomena, passing wind, burping and snoring tend to make us feel awkward or embarrassed. Do we feel embarrassed when we cough? If not, why is it that we are embarrassed with passing wind, burping and snoring?

24. Thoughts

What thoughts do you hold
Good thoughts or bad?
Are you lost in the ways of life,
Of yesterday's trials and tribulations?

Does your mind fancy a break –
A break from routine,
Boredom and life?
Have years travelled far?

The thought of the apple falling down
Made the farmer Newton a scientist.
So did a tub filled with water
Make Archimedes a scientist.

Profound thoughts did Chaucer,
Milton and Shakespeare
Engrave in literature.
So did Chomsky and Dennett.

My thoughts are not of a scientist,
Philosopher or a doctor
But of a common man
Whose thoughts clutter with good and bad.

Thoughts of innovation, chores and routine
Thoughts that keep me going
Thoughts that make me carve an identity
Thoughts unique and distinct to my identity.

Inspiration or thought:
Thoughts

Thoughts drive the human mind. It is a mental activity that makes us who we are. Profound thoughts have led to innovations and discoveries. Whether we are innovators or regular people, we all have thoughts. They are distinct and similar at the same time. The distinctiveness of thoughts makes one stand out from the others, while similar thoughts, when grouped together, form the collective thought-process of the masses.

25. Two Logs of Wood

The sea breeze kissed me
And woke me up from my sleep.
The sea is rough
So are the waves.
The dandelions swayed around
The white lilies on me dried up
So did the red roses.
The funeral service is long over.
As weeks, months and years pass by
Visitors stopped;
I have become a memory
Framed in glass.
Moths and worms ate me up
The fine linen is no more
I am but a skeleton
Sandwiched between two logs of wood.

The degrees and accolades
The laurels I claimed
Assets I bought
Wealth I accumulated
Are far and distant.
I heard a cry every month
There is a new neighbour every month.

I smiled
In months they too will lose their visitors,
For I know I have already lost them.
Next to me lie
Writers and lawyers
Doctors, policemen and artists
Cleaners, plumbers and firemen.
We share
Memories far and near
Have a laugh,
Shed a tear,
Moan in sorrow and pain.

The lilies and roses
Stopped.
We lost visitors as years passed
Some joined us to give us company,
Others lost interest.
Ponder did I
What a second chance meant.
Three meals did I want
A roof to sleep under,
People to love and live with,
To have them visit my tombstone.
The time has come
For my soul to depart the body
I know not
If I have enough friends
To remember me
When I lie beneath my tombstone.

Inspiration or thought: Two Logs of Wood

We are all part of a busy rat race. We have become too busy for each other. We are either working hard to earn a livelihood, or we are taking care of our family. Time has become so precious that we are hardly able to spend it with family and friends. "Two Logs of Wood" is a reminder to the human race that when we lie beneath the ground, we do not take anything along with us, and all that we leave behind is a legacy. It is important that we pause and ask ourselves what life will be after we die. Will anyone visit our tombstones years after our burial?

Thank you very much for taking time to read my poems.

9 7 9 8 8 8 9 2 2 2 1 6 9 6